The GROSS AND GOOFY Body

Germ Wars!

The Secrets of Protecting Your Body

By Melissa Stewart

Illustrated by Janet Hamlin

mc Marshall Cavendish
Benchmark
New York

**THIS BOOK WAS MADE POSSIBLE,
IN PART, BY A GRANT FROM THE
SOCIETY OF CHILDREN'S BOOK WRITERS AND ILLUSTRATORS.**

Text copyright © 2011 Melissa Stewart
Illustrations copyright © 2011 Marshall Cavendish Corporation

Published by Marshall Cavendish Benchmark
An imprint of Marshall Cavendish Corporation

This publication represents the opinions and views of the author based on Melissa Stewart's personal experience, knowledge, and research. The information in this book serves as a general guide only. The author and publisher have used their best efforts in preparing this book and disclaim liability rising directly and indirectly from the use and application of this book.

Other Marshall Cavendish Offices:
Marshall Cavendish International (Asia) Private Limited, 1 New Industrial Road, Singapore 536196 • Marshall Cavendish International (Thailand) Co Ltd. 253 Asoke, 12th Flr, Sukhumvit 21 Road, Klongtoey Nua, Wattana, Bangkok 10110, Thailand • Marshall Cavendish (Malaysia) Sdn Bhd, Times Subang, Lot 46, Subang Hi-Tech Industrial Park, Batu Tiga, 40000 Shah Alam, Selangor Darul Ehsan, Malaysia

Marshall Cavendish is a trademark of Times Publishing Limited

All websites were available and accurate when this book was sent to press.

Library of Congress Cataloging-in-Publication Data
Stewart, Melissa.
Germ wars! : the secrets of protecting your body / Melissa Stewart.
p. cm. — (The gross and goofy body)
Includes index.
Summary: "Provides comprehensive information on the role the immune system plays in the body science of humans and animals"—Provided by the publisher.
ISBN 978-0-7614-4165-6
1. Immune system—Juvenile literature. 2. Immunity—Juvenile literature.
3. Bacteria—Juvenile literature. I. Title.
QR181.8.S77 2009
571.9'6—dc22
2008033562

Editor: Joy Bean
Publisher: Michelle Bisson
Art Director: Anahid Hamparian
Series Designer: Daniel Roode

Photo research by Tracey Engel
Cover photo: Gabrielle Revere/Taxi/Getty Images

The photographs in this book are used by permission and through the courtesy of:
Getty Images: Taxi/Wendy Ashton, 5 (bottom); Visuals Unlimited/Jerome Wexler, 7 (top); GAP Photos/Carole Drake, 7 (bottom); Visuals Unlimited/Science VU, 8; Riser/flashfilm, 13 (top); The Image Bank/Stephen Schauer, 13 (bottom); The Image Bank/SMC Images, 15 (top, right); Visuals Unlimited/Dr. Dennis Kunkel, 15 (top, left); Stone/Asger Carlsen, 16; Gallo Images/Anthony Bannister, 17 (right); Taxi/Brian Kenney, 17 (left); Stone/Elyse Lewin, 19 (top); DK Stock/Kevin RL Hanson, 22; Stone/Ryan McVay, 23 (bottom); Iconica/Frans Lemmens , 25 (top); Visuals Unlimited/Brandon Cole, 25 (bottom); Taxi/Gabrielle Revere, 26; 3D Clinic, 28; Visuals Unlimited/Dr. David Phillips, 29 (bottom); Photographer's Choice/Michael Dunning , 31 (top); Visuals Unlimited/Bill Beatty, 33 (top); Visuals Unlimited/Alex Kerstitch, 33 (bottom); Visuals Unlimited/Dr. Fred Hossler, 38; LOOK/Holger Leue , 39 (top); Photographer's Choice/artpartner-images, 40 (bottom, right). *Photo Researchers, Inc.:* Brian Evans, 21 (top); CNRI, 34 (right); Dr P. Marazzi, 37 (bottom).

Printed in Malaysia (T)
135642

CONTENTS

DUTIFUL DEFENDERS

"Go ahead," whispers your brother. "I dare you."

So you pour a pile of pepper into your hand, hold it under your nose, and breathe deeply. After all, who can resist a dare?

Your nose starts to tingle, tickle, and twitch. Then suddenly, you feel it—deep down in your chest. Muscles are pushing a blast of air up and out, and there's nothing you can do.

"Aaaah CHOO!"

Sneezing is your nose's way of ousting irritating invaders—such as pepper, dust, **germs**, and even itty-bitty bugs. It's just one of many built-in defense systems that protects your delicate insides and keeps you healthy.

What are your body's other dutiful defenders? The answer might surprise you. They include earwax, vomit, boogers, spit, and more. You'll be amazed at all the ways these bodacious bodyguards make life better for you—and for other animals, too.

When it comes to barfing, frogs are real pros. A frog throws up its whole stomach, scoops out the chewed-up chunks of food, and then swallows its stomach back down.

When a mouse licks a wound, chemicals in its spit attack germs.

Don't worry if your pet iguana sneezes. It's just getting rid of extra salts that have built up inside its body.

TINY TRESPASSERS

Your skin. It's like a protective suit of armor that covers every inch of your body—from head to toe. Or does it?

Your nose and mouth are open to the outside world. So are your ears and eyes. And that can be a problem. Just about anything floating or flying through the air can sneak into the holes in your head. The tiny trespassers include bits of dirt, dust and sand,

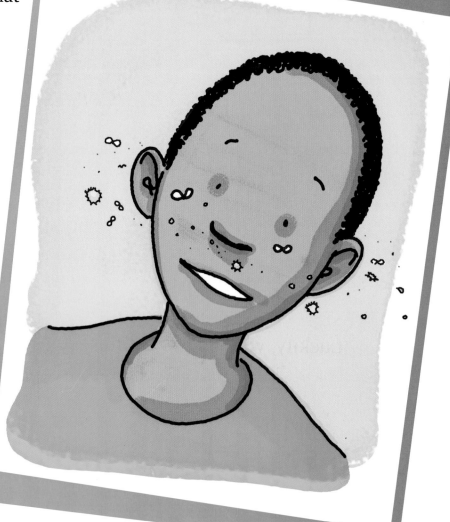

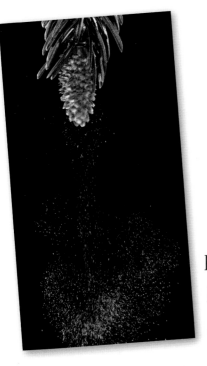

powdery pollen from plants, small insects, germs, even particles from outer space! Believe it or not, these little guys can cause big problems. They can clog your nose and make it hard to breathe. They can damage your eyeballs and make it hard to see. Some of them can even make you sick.

Luckily, your body's dutiful defenders are always ready for action. And they have just one message for tiny troublemakers: "Get out and stay out!"

A Parade of Pollen

How many species, or kinds, of plants do you think grow in your neighborhood? Each one makes its own pollen. The powdery stuff might not bother you, but it makes some people feel as if they have a cold.

GERMS ARE EVERYWHERE!

Germs as seen through
a microscope, magnified
300,000 times.

You've seen smoke and sand, dust, and itty-bitty insects, but have you ever seen a germ? Of course not! Germs are way too small. You need a microscope to see them.

Maybe it's a good thing that germs are invisible. After all, they're everywhere—in the air you breathe, on the food you eat, and in the water you drink.

About 7 billion people live on Earth today. But there are more germs than that on and inside your body right now.

Germs are on your skin and under your fingernails.

They're inside your mouth, nose, and intestines.

They're even on your eyelashes.

How would you feel if you could see all those tiny critters?

There are four kinds of germs—bacteria, viruses, fungi, and protozoa. Most of them don't bother you a bit. But some germs can be deadly.

Dare to Compare

Just how small are germs? To find out, grab an apple and prick its skin with a pin. A cluster of a million bacteria could easily slip through that hole.

Viruses are even smaller. If the average virus were the size of your apple, an average bacterium would be the size of a giraffe.

9

WHO DONE IT?

When doctors see sick patients, they act like police detectives trying to solve a crime. They ask lots of questions and run tests to find out who done it. Here's what you should know about their suspects.

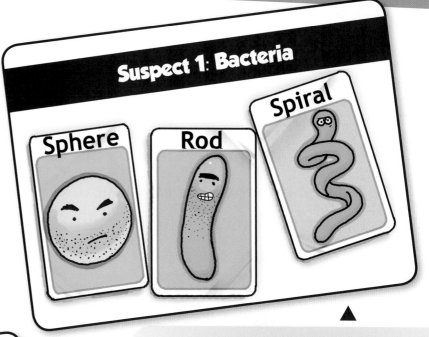

Suspect 1: Bacteria

Sphere

Rod

Spiral

Description: Tiny, one-celled living things that reproduce by splitting in half. They can be shaped like spheres, long thin rods, or spirals.
Known Crimes: Acne, ear infections, food poisoning, Lyme disease, strep throat, tooth decay

Suspect 2: Viruses

Ah-Choo

Description: Teeny-tiny particles that most scientists say aren't alive. They invade the cells of living things and force them to crank out hundreds of new viruses. When a cell is full of viruses, it explodes. The viruses burst out and attack new cells.
Known Crimes: Chicken pox, common cold, flu, food poisoning, warts

Description: One-celled or multicelled living things. Their bodies are made of thin threads that branch out in every direction. The threads absorb, or take in, nutrients from a fungus's surroundings. Fungi that can make you sick include molds and yeasts.
Known Crimes: Athlete's foot, food poisoning, ringworm

Suspect 3: Fungi

Suspect 4: Protozoa

Description: Small, one-celled living things that can move on their own and feed on even smaller creatures. They are common in dirty water.
Known Crimes: African sleeping sickness, giardiasis, malaria

THE HISTORY OF GERMS

Humans have lived on Earth for more than 250,000 years. But for most of that time, we didn't even know that germs existed.

People finally caught their first glimpses of germs in the 1600s. But it took another two hundred years for scientists and doctors to realize that germs can cause disease.

In the late 1800s, scientists began to figure out which germs cause which diseases. Then they looked for ways to stop the deadly invaders. Through the years, germ researchers have made many important discoveries, and their hard work continues today.

1595 The light microscope is invented in Holland. ▶

1670s Antoni van Leeuwenhoek, a Dutchman, looks at spit under a microscope. He sees "little, living animacules, very prettily a-moving [in] such enormous numbers, that all the water . . . seemed to be alive." Leeuwenhoek's "animacules" are bacteria, but he doesn't know they can cause disease.

1845 German scientist Karl Siebold publishes a book describing many different kinds of protozoa.

1857 French scientist Louis Pasteur suggests that tiny germs make us sick. Most people laugh at the idea.

1865 British surgeon Joseph Lister reads Pasteur's paper and thinks it makes sense. He begins cleaning his equipment and bandages in a liquid that kills germs. He sprays a germ-killing antiseptic on his surgical clothes and on patient's wounds.

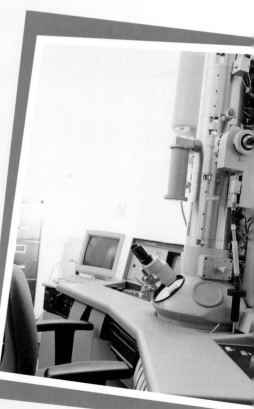

1869 Thanks to his germ-killing techniques, Lister's patient survival rate increases from about 50 percent to 88 percent.

1935 American scientists use a new invention—the electron microscope—to see viruses for the first time. ▶

1957 American scientist Robert Whittaker realizes that fungi are not plants. They are a separate group of living things.

GERM POWER

Which is more dangerous: two huge human armies or one tiny germ?

Seems like a no-brainer, right? But don't answer too fast. First, get the facts.

Between 1914 and 1918, many countries fought in World War I. By the time the Allied Powers (led by Great Britain, France, and the United States) finally defeated the Central Powers (led by Germany, Austria-Hungary, and Turkey), about 20 million people had died.

Just as the war was ending, Spanish flu swept across Europe. It killed 25 million people in 6 months. That's one gruesome germ!

Why can germs do so much damage? Because they reproduce very quickly. Some bacteria divide every twenty minutes. In just three days, one of them could produce enough new bacteria to equal the mass of the entire Earth. Thank goodness your body's dutiful defenders are constantly battling the bad guys.

How Many Germs

Almost every illness you can think of is caused by a germ. Scientists have identified at least 5,000 kinds of viruses and 30,000 kinds of bacteria. There are probably thousands more left to discover.

Germ vs. Germ

Believe it or not, some kinds of viruses attack and destroy bacteria.

IN THE BLINK OF AN EYE

When the wind hurls sand in your face or a curious insect gets a little too close, your eyelids snap shut. An instant later, they spring back open. With each blink, your eyelashes flick away the little troublemakers.

How can your eyelids flit so fast? Because the muscle that blinks them is the fastest muscle in your whole body. It's also one of the hardest working. Most of the time, you blink thirty to sixty times a minute. That adds up to about thirty thousand times a day and more than ten million times a year.

Some animals don't have eyelids. Some have two—just like you. And some animals have three. Their extra eyelid is called a haw. It opens and closes sideways, and animals can see through it.

An aardvark's haws keep ants and termites out of its eyes.

While a woodpecker jackhammers a tree, it closes its haws to protect its eyes from flying bits of wood.

Sometimes hungry eaglets accidentally jab their parents' eyes as they lunge for food. That's why adult eagles slam their haws shut before feeding their young.

THE EYES HAVE IT!

Eyelids are fast, but sometimes they aren't quite quick enough. Luckily, your eyes have an emergency back-up system—tears.

Like the water slowly dripping out of a leaky faucet, your body is constantly cranking out a fresh supply of tears. They're made inside tear glands, small sacs located above your eyes.

Most days about 1/3 of a teaspoon (1.7 milliliters) of new tears trickle into each eye. Some of the watery liquid evaporates. It turns into a gas and rises into the air. The rest drains into tear ducts, tiny tubes that run between your eyes and nose.

If a bit of dirt or sand lands in your eye, your tear glands work overtime. They make extra tears to wash away the pesky particles.

Slip and Slide

There's a good reason tears look like water. Water is their main ingredient. But tears also contain salts and germ-killing chemicals. Sometimes supersneaky viruses and bacteria manage to slip past the germ killers. Then they slide into your body through a tear duct.

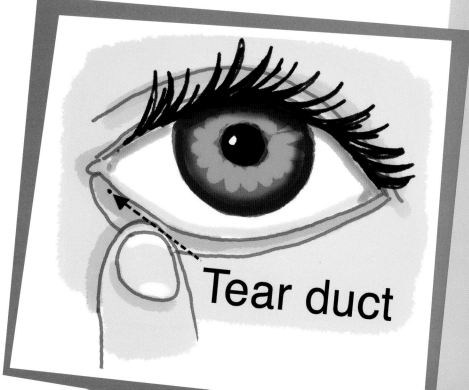

Tear duct

See for Yourself

Stand in front of a mirror and gently pull down the inside corner of your lower eyelid. See that tiny hole? It's your tear duct.

IN YOUR EAR!

Just like your eyes, your ears open to the outside world. So it's a good thing that icky earwax coats your ear canal. Earwax protects your ears' most delicate parts by trapping anything that flies, crawls, or gets blown inside. And like tears, earwax contains chemicals that kill most germs.

Earwax is made in dozens of cerumen glands that surround your ear canal.

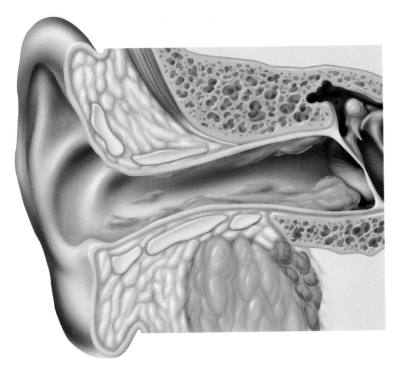

It oozes through tiny tubes and slowly seeps into your ear canal. Newly made earwax pushes older earwax out of the way. Like lumpy oatmeal on a conveyor belt, aged earwax and its load of garbage slowly slides out of your ear.

If your earwax is dry and flaky, it falls out of your ear. If it's wet and sticky, you rinse it away as you wash your hair.

Clumps or Flakes?

Your spit looks just like everyone else's spit. So does your snot and eye goop. So you probably think that everyone's earwax looks the same, too. But think again.

Some people have soft, sticky earwax that forms yellow clumps. These people have ancestors who came from Europe or Africa. Other people have hard, crusty, gray flakes. They have ancestors who were Asian or American Indian.

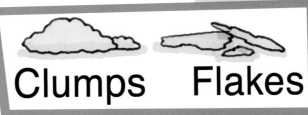

Clumps   Flakes

UP YOUR NOSE!

Take a deep breath, but don't let it out—at least not right away.

While you're holding in all that air, consider this: it's chock full of irritating invaders. They could damage your nasal passages or make you sick. So what does your nose do? It protects itself.

Your nose's first line of defense is the hundreds of small, stiff hairs just inside your nostrils. Want to see them? It's easy. Just hold a mirror under your nose. If you're really lucky, you might even see stuff stuck in the hairs. Ew! Gross!

When you breathe out, the junk trapped in your nose hairs gets blasted back into the air.

Nose hairs don't stop all the pesky pests that get sucked into your schnoz. But don't worry. Your nifty nose and the rest of your respiratory system have lots of other self-cleaning tricks.

Hairy and Scary

Ever noticed dark, wiry hairs dangling out of your dad's nose? Take a look at dinner tonight.

As men get older, their nose hairs sometimes grow a little too long. But luckily, there's any easy solution. Just grab some small scissors and snip, snip!

STOP THAT STUFF!

Most of the itty-bitty invaders that whiz past your nose hairs crash into your nasal passages. They get stuck in an icky, sticky slime we call snot.

Most snot is produced by cells on the surface of your nasal passages. In just one day, you make enough snot to fill a 1-liter (34-ounce) soda bottle.

Snot surrounds dirt, germs, and other pesky particles. Over time, the mixture dries and hardens into a solid booger. Some boogers are soft and squishy. Others are tough and crumbly. But they can all hold their shape.

When a big, juicy booger tickles the inside of your nose, you might be tempted to pick it. But don't do it! Poking around up there can give you a bloody nose.

Snot is one kind of mucus—a thick, gummy goo that animals use in all kinds of ways.

The mucus on a tree frog's toes helps it stick to branches and other rough surfaces.

The mucus on an African chameleon's tongue is perfect for catching tasty insects.

When **predators** attack, a hagfish slimes them with mucus. The sticky goo traps the enemies while the hagfish escapes.

WHAT A BLAST!

When tiny trespassers smash into nerve cells on the surface of your nasal passages, a warning signal rushes to your brain. Then your body's boss sends out a message telling muscles in your chest to squeeze. Before you know it, you're sneezing up a storm.

Each sneeze thrusts about 40,000 tiny droplets of spit and snot out of your body. The spray explodes out of your nose and mouth at speeds of up to 150 miles (241 kilometers) per hour and may travel as far as 30 feet (9 meters). It's a quick, easy way to get irritating invaders out of your body.

Why do people say "Bless you !" when you sneeze? Because sneezing is often the first sign of sickness. Here's what well-wishers in other parts of the world say when someone sneezes:

Salve!

Gesundheidt!

Country	Saying	What It Means
ITALY	"Salve!"	"Good health to you!"
GERMANY	"Gesundheit!"	"Health!"
SAUDI ARABIA	"Alhamdulillah!"	"Praise be to God!"
RUSSIA	"Bud zdorov!"	"Be healthy!"
CHINA	"Bai sui!"	"May you live one hundred years!"

Bai sui!

THE FINAL WEAPON

Just like nose hairs, snot and sneezing stop lots of tiny troublemakers. But these battling bodyguards can't stop them all.

Some particles and germs sneak all the way through your nasal passages. Then they whiz down your throat and enter your trachea, or windpipe.

Just like your nose, your trachea produces a steady supply of sticky, icky mucus. We call it phlegm.

Your bronchi, the tubes that enter your lungs, make phlegm, too. So do your lungs. Phlegm is your body's final weapon against the invaders that threaten your delicate lungs.

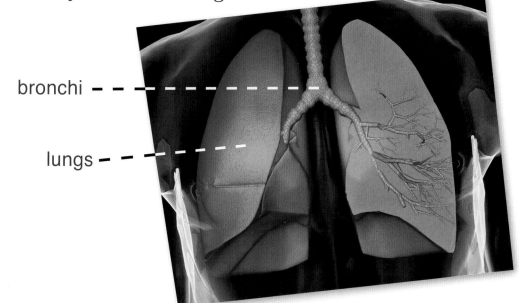

bronchi

lungs

Most of the time, teeny, tiny hairs called cilia sweep phlegm and the junk stuck in it up to your throat so you can swallow it. But when you have a cold, your respiratory system goes into mucus-making overdrive, and your cilia can't keep up.

What do you do to get rid of the gooey gobs and slippery slime? You cough it out into the world.

Hack Attack

When you cough, air bursts out of your body at speeds of up to 760 miles (1,223 km) per hour. Sometimes people cough so hard that they break one of their ribs.

Cilia, such as the ones shown here in blue, line the surface of your throat.

OPEN WIDE

Whenever you talk, eat, smile, or yawn, you open your mouth to the outside world. That gives particles in the air plenty of chances to float inside.

But that's not the only way tiny trespassers sneak into your mouth. They're also on and inside the food you eat. And the minute germs enter your mouth, they start to multiply. Believe it or not, there could be as many as 50 billion bacteria living in your mouth right now.

Luckily, your spit—or saliva as doctors and scientists call it—is hard at work. It's washing your tongue and gums. It's rinsing bits of food out of your teeth. And the germ-killing chemicals in your saliva are attacking the bacteria that cause bad breath and tooth decay. Thank goodness for spit!

Bacteria Buddies

A komodo dragon's saliva is teeming with harmful bacteria, but the world's largest lizard doesn't mind a bit. When the hungry hunter bites into prey, the germs in its mouth infect the victim's wounds. If the injured animal manages to escape, the komodo dragon follows it until it dies.

Words of Wisdom

A wise man once said, "Never spit into the wind, or the wind will spit back at you." Sounds like good advice.

UP AND OUT!

Puke. Barf. Vomit.
Ralph. Boot. Hurl.
Upchuck.
Spew chunks.
Toss your cookies.

Nobody likes throwing up—the burning throat, the stinking stench, the kneeling in front of the toilet. It's no fun at all. But vomiting is one of the ways your body gets rid of harmful germs.

Every time you swallow, the germs floating in your spit are swept down your esophagus and into your stomach. Within minutes, digestive juices destroy the little pests.

But sometimes germs arrive hidden inside chunks of chewed-up food. If your stomach senses these unwanted visitors, it sends a warning to your brain. Then your brain sends a message to the muscles in your stomach and esophagus, "Up and out!"

Before you know it, your lunch is in your lap. Ugh! What a mess!

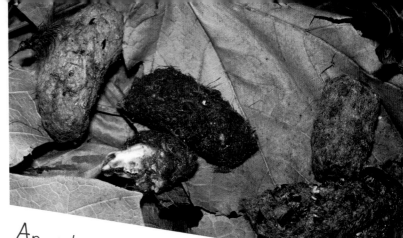

An owl vomits after every meal. All the undigestible parts of its **prey**—fur, bones, teeth—get packed into a pellet and hurled out of its body.

A whale vomits the materials it can't digest about once a week.

When an enemy attacks, a sea cucumber throws up its stomach. That's enough to scare off most predators.

SQUIRT ALERT!

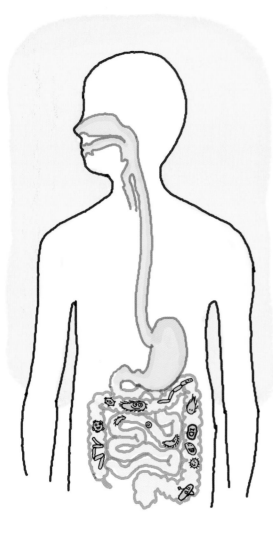

Sometimes your stomach doesn't notice germs, and they make it all the way to your intestines. Then the irritating invaders get pushed out your back end in a hurry.

Mashed-up food particles usually spend about six hours in your small intestine. During that time, nutrients move into your bloodstream.

Then, the undigestible leftovers move into your large intestine. For the next eighteen hours, muscles squeeze water out of the mangled mash to form dry, lumpy poop.

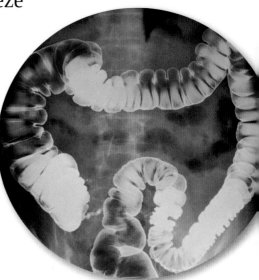

But if your intestines detect germs, there's an immediate change in plans. Instead of taking the time to remove nutrients and water, your intestines thrust the wet, smelly mush forward. And it blasts out your butt as diarrhea.

Facts About Flow

Sometimes a smooth, steady stream of diarrhea flows out of your body. Sometimes diarrhea comes out in dribbling drips. And once in a while it explodes out of your anus—the hole at the end of your digestive tract—along with blasts of gas. It all depends on what kind of germs you've eaten, the kind of food it was in, and how quickly your body wants to get rid of the irritating invaders.

HOORAY FOR BLOOD!

You fall off your bike and land on your knee. Ouch! That hurts.

But the pain isn't your biggest problem.

Scratches and scrapes crisscross your knee. Each one is like an open door for dirt, bacteria, and other pesky pests.

Luckily, your body knows just what to do.

Blood slowly leaks out of the largest scratches, but don't worry. It only takes a few minutes for the trickle to stop. And in the meantime, lots of tiny troublemakers go with the flow. That's right—the flood of blood helps clean out your cuts.

And as your hardworking heart pumps blood through your body, thousands of white blood cells arrive on the scene and get to work. These jellylike blobs are always ready to battle the bad guys. Some track down tiny bits of dirt and gobble them up. Others attack bacteria that have sneaked into your wound.

Signs of Trouble

Have a cut that's red and swollen? That means bacteria and white blood cells are battling it out. See a clump of goopy pus inside your wound? It's the piled-up bodies of dead white blood cells. Yuck!

THE WHITE WARRIORS

Your eyelids and tears, earwax and mucus, vomit and diarrhea, spit and sneezes catch millions of germs and hurl them out of your body. But these dutiful defenders can't stop all the tiny trespassers that get inside you.

Luckily, white blood cells do more than just clean out your cuts. They also fight the germs that cause colds, the flu, and just about every other illness you can think of. Good thing your body produces about 100 billion new white blood cells every single day.

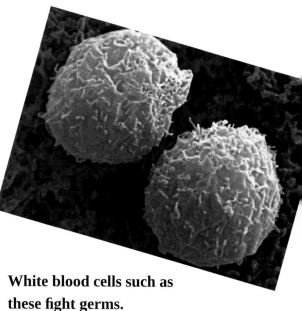

Some white blood cells remember the invaders your body has fought in the past. If the same germ attacks again, these white blood cells quickly crank out an army of antibodies—proteins that seek out and destroy a specific invader.

White blood cells such as these fight germs.

38

Laughter Really Is the Best Medicine

Want to stay healthy? Have a good laugh—and that's no joke. When you laugh, giggle, or snort, your body produces more germ-fighting white blood cells. It also cranks out extra antibodies, so irritating invaders don't stand a chance.

Aging Antibodies

Ever noticed that you get sick more often than your parents do? That's because adults have more antibodies to fight off germs.

CRIME STOPPERS

A bloody bandage.
A puddle of vomit.
A snotty tissue.
A wad of earwax.
An envelope sealed with spit.

What do all these things have in common? They contain DNA—the genetic material inside your cells. It codes for height, eye color, and other body traits. Like fingerprints, everyone's DNA is different. That means police can use it to help solve crimes.

Even when police can't find fingerprints at a crime scene, they often find traces of DNA. Police in the United States have used DNA evidence to investigate murders and other violent crimes for many years. In 2006, they began analyzing DNA evidence in less serious crimes, including car thefts and house robberies. Criminals beware!

From fighting crime and battling germs to keeping our eyes, ears, noses, and mouths safe and clean, it's hard to believe all the ways our body's built-in defense systems protect us every day. And we aren't alone. Every living thing has its own loyal legion of dutiful defenders.

Did You Know?

You can't catch a cold from a dog or cat, but you can get the flu from a horse, a pig, or even a duck.

antibody—A protein that is programmed to find and destroy a specific bacteria or virus.

antiseptic—A substance that destroys germs.

anus—The hole at the end of the digestive tract.

bacterium (pl. bacteria)—A tiny, one-celled living thing that reproduces by dividing.

bronchus (pl. bronchi)—A tube that connects the trachea with one of the lungs.

cerumen gland—A tiny sac that produces and releases cerumen, or earwax.

cilium (pl. cilia)—A tiny hair. Cilia in the respiratory system sweep snot, mucus, and phlegm containing invading particles to the esophagus or mouth.

DNA (deoxyribonucleic acid)—A molecule with instructions that direct all the activities in a cell. It is passed from parent to child during reproduction.

ear canal—The tube that leads from outside the ear to the eardrum.

esophagus—The tube that connects the pharynx with the stomach.

evaporate—To change from a liquid to a gas.

fungus (pl. fungi)— A one-celled or multicelled living thing. Its body is made of thin threads that absorb nutrients.

germ—A tiny organism or particle that can make you sick.

haw—A third eyelid located below the outer eyelids. It is transparent and opens and closes sideways, instead of up and down.

intestine—The part of the digestive system that allows nutrients to pass into the blood and removes water from the undigestible leftovers. Scientists often divide it into two sections—the small intestine and the large intestine.

mucus—A slimy mixture that coats many surfaces inside the body. In the respiratory system it stops germs, dirt, pollen, and other foreign particles from reaching the lungs.

nasal passage—One of the tunnels inside the nose. Air travels through nasal passages on its way to your trachea.

nerve cell—A neuron; a cell that carries messages to and from the brain.

nostril—One of the holes at the bottom of the nose.

nutrient—A substance that keeps the body healthy. It comes from food.

phlegm—Mucus produced in the lungs.

pollen—A powdery material released from plants. It floats in the air and can irritate the nose.

predator—An animal that hunts and kills other animals for food.

prey—An animal that is hunted by a predator.

protozoan (pl. protozoa)—A small, one-celled living thing that can move on its own and feeds on even smaller creatures.

respiratory system—The group of body organs that takes in oxygen and gets rid of carbon dioxide.

saliva—A watery liquid containing gases, salts, mucus, and proteins that breaks down food and destroys bacteria living in your mouth. It is also called spit.

tear duct—A tube that drains tears out of the eye. It connects to the nose.

tear gland—A tiny sac that produces and releases tears.

trachea—The tube that connects the lungs with the throat.

virus—A tiny particle that most scientists say isn't alive. Viruses invade the cells of living things and force them to crank out hundreds of new viruses.

white blood cell—A blood cell that defends the body against bacteria, viruses, and other invaders.

A NOTE ON SOURCES

Dear Readers,

I went to some pretty strange places to research this book, including my bathroom, the grocery store, and even an animal hospital. But my first stop was the library. That's where I found college-level textbooks on anatomy and physiology.

Once I had a general overview of the topic, I read more focused articles in scientific journals, newspapers, and magazines. That's how I discovered that laughing boosts your immune system and that police are now using DNA from snot, vomit, spit, and earwax to solve crimes. I also learned about the history of studying germs.

Some of the best information about animal defense systems came from books. I also searched for fun facts on the Internet. That's how I found out that the Spanish flu killed more people than World War I.

My final step was to speak to scientists doing research on the immune and digestive systems. These interviews ensure that the book includes the most up-to-date information about germs that cause food poisoning and how wounds heal.

—Melissa Stewart

BOOKS

Amazing Animals of the World. New York: Scholastic Library, 2006.

Nye, Bill. *Great Big Book of Tiny Germs.* New York: Hyperion, 2005.

Simon, Seymour. *Guts: Our Digestive System.* New York: HarperCollins, 2005.

Solway, Andrew. *The Respiratory System.* Chicago: World Book, Inc., 2007.

WEBSITES

Guinness World Records
This site contains up-to-date information on some of the strangest world records you can imagine.
http://www.guinnessworldrecords.com/default.aspx

That Explains It!
This site contains all kinds of interesting information about the human body, animals, food, inventions and machines, and more.
http://www.coolquiz.com/trivia/explain/

INDEX

Page numbers in bold are illustrations.

ABOUT THE AUTHOR

Melissa Stewart has written everything from board books for preschoolers to magazine articles for adults. She is the award-winning author of more than one hundred books for young readers. She serves on the board of advisors of the Society of Children's Book Writers and Illustrators and is a judge for the American Institute of Physics Children's Science Writing Award. Stewart earned a B.S. in biology from Union College and an M.A. in science journalism from New York University. She lives in Acton, Massachusetts, with her husband, Gerard. To learn more about Stewart, please visit her website: www.melissa-stewart.com.

ABOUT THE ILLUSTRATOR

Janet Hamlin has illustrated many children's books, games, newspapers, and even Harry Potter stuff. She is also a court artist. The Gross and Goofy Body is one of her all-time favorite series, and she now considers herself the factoid queen of bodily functions. She lives and draws in New York and loves it.